Morton Gould

GHOST WALTZES

for Piano

duration: ca. 11 minutes

ED-3865
First Printing: May 1992

G. SCHIRMER, *Inc.*

DISTRIBUTED BY
HAL•LEONARD™
CORPORATION
7777 W. BLUEMOUND RD. P.O. BOX 13819 MILWAUKEE, WI 53213

The first musical sounds I heard in my early years came from my parents' player piano. The music on those piano rolls reflected the taste of that period, with a preponderance of waltzes of all kinds—Viennese, Russian, American, Chopin, Strauss, etc. This piece, therefore, is a distillation of these dance forms in three-quarter time—nostalgic, poignant, assertive, reflective, brash, sentimental, celebrative, elegiac. It is a fantasy collage of my waltz memories filtered through time, with haunting "pianola" sounds intertwining throughout. I thought it appropriate for the Van Cliburn International Piano Competition to attempt a virtuosic piece that enables the performer to rhapsodize these many contrasting textures and moods that are unique to the waltz.

—MORTON GOULD

Commissioned for the ninth Van Cliburn International Piano Competition (1993) by Mr. Lewis F. Kornfeld, Jr., in memory of his wife, Ethel Hardy Kornfeld.

for the ninth Van Cliburn International Piano Competition

GHOST WALTZES

Morton Gould
1991

Moderato ♩ = 100

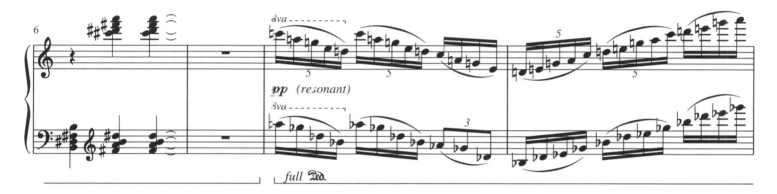

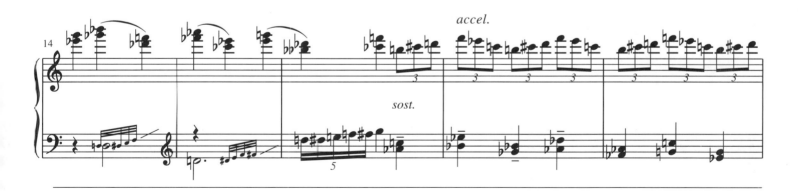

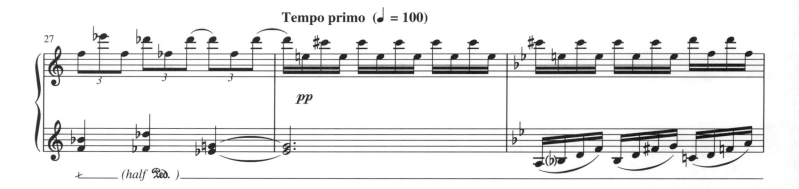

rit. poco a poco

Tempo primo ($\quarternote$ = 100)

pp

(half Ped.)

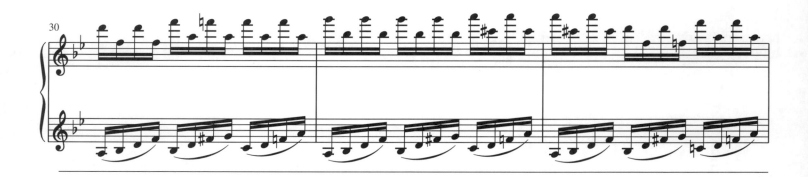

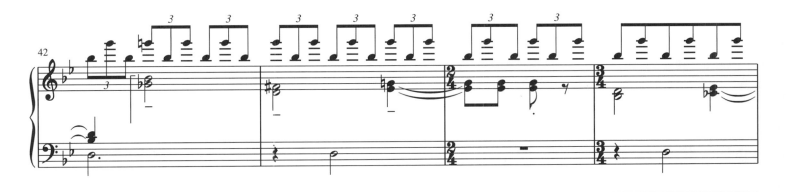

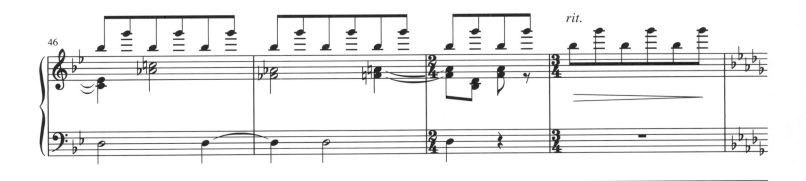

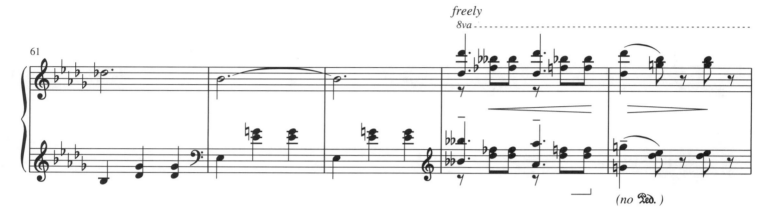

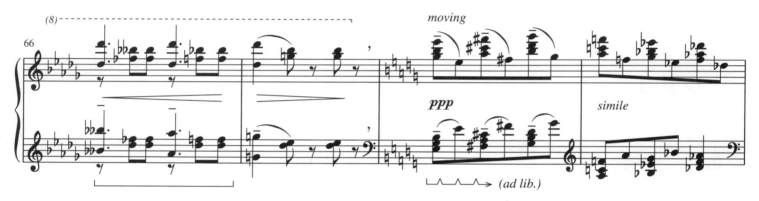

A tempo ♩ = 72

Meno mosso ♩ = 50
Sostenuto, broadly

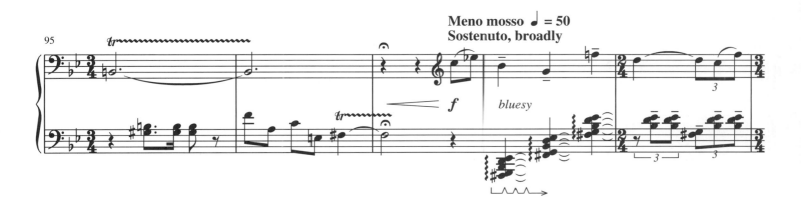

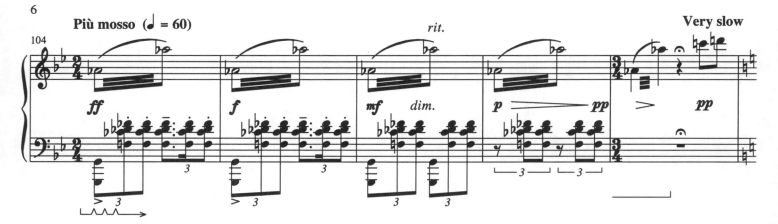

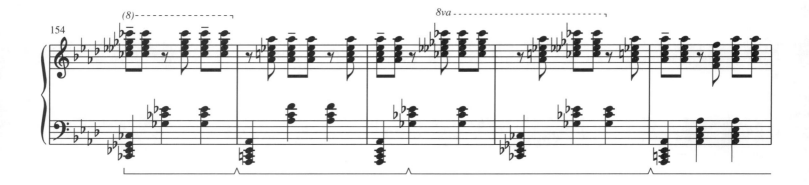

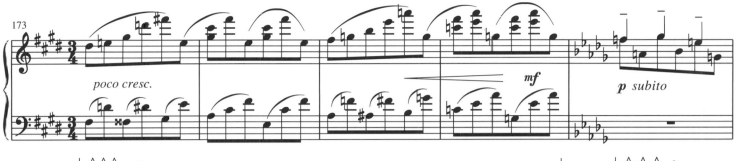

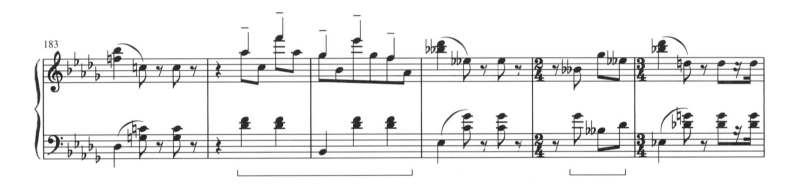

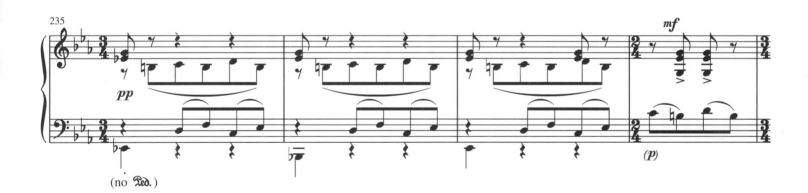

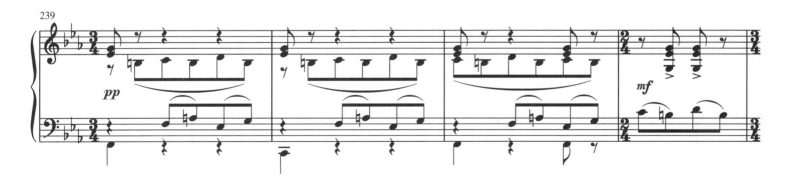

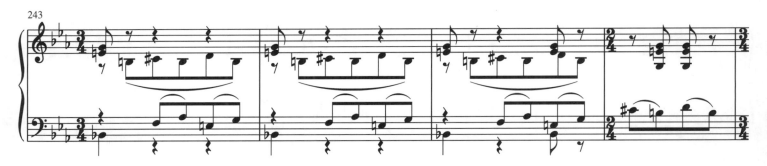

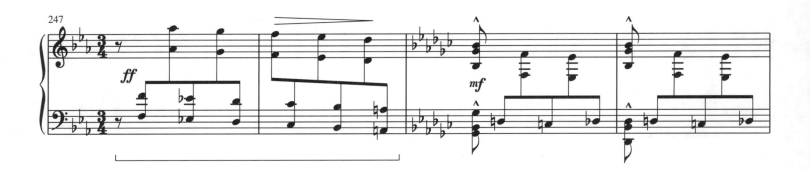

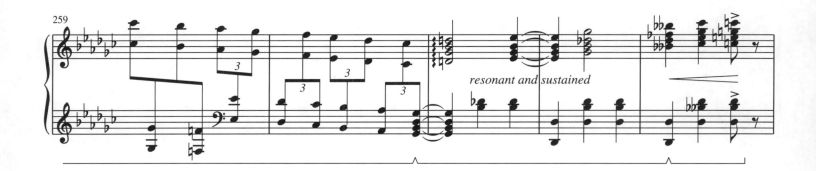

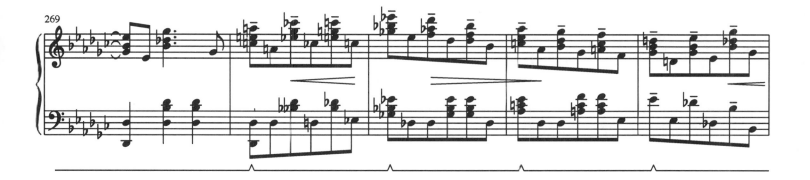

Meno mosso - rubato

(3+2) Meno mosso—pesante

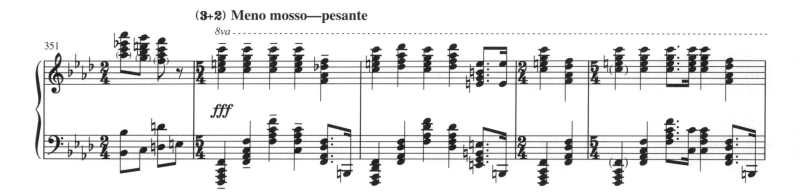

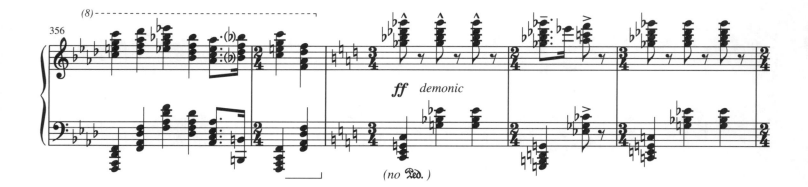

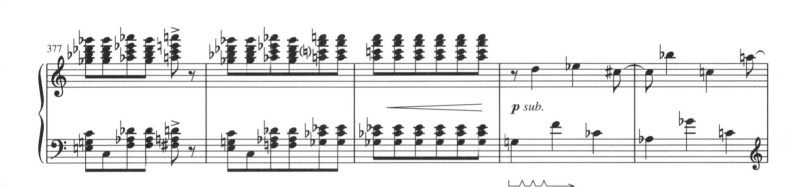

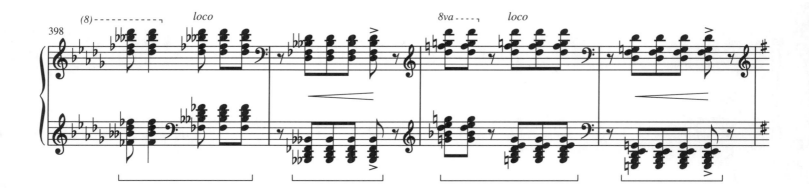

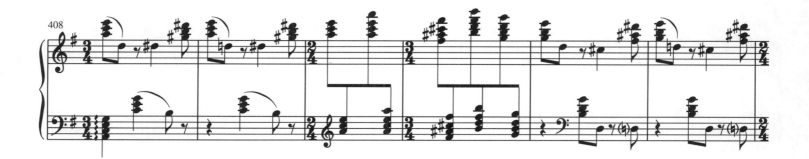

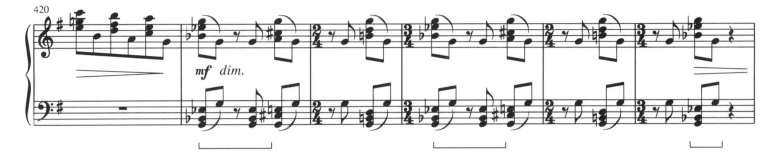

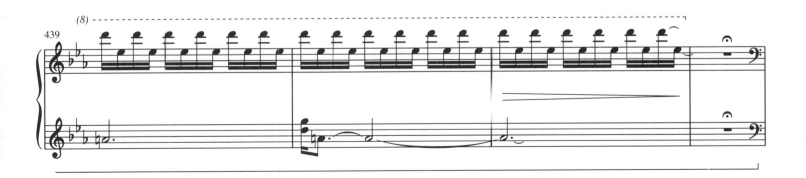

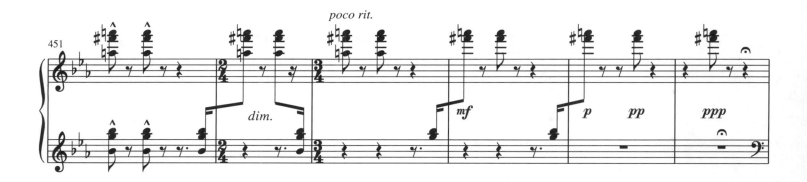